MOVERS, SHAKERS, & HISTORY MAKERS

SCOTT KELLY
ASTRONAUT TWIN WHO SPENT A YEAR IN SPACE

CONTENT CONSULTANT
JON G. STELLER, MD
SPACE MEDICINE AND REPRODUCTIVE HEALTH RESEARCHER
MATERNAL FETAL MEDICINE, UNIVERSITY OF CALIFORNIA, IRVINE

BY ANNA SAXTON

CAPSTONE PRESS
a capstone imprint

Capstone Captivate is published by Capstone Press, an imprint of Capstone.
1710 Roe Crest Drive
North Mankato, Minnesota 56003
www.capstonepub.com

Library of Congress Cataloging-in-Publication Data
Names: Saxton, Anna, author.
Title: Scott Kelly : astronaut twin who spent a year in space / Anna
    Saxton.
Description: North Mankato, MN : Capstone Press, 2021. | Series: Movers,
    shakers, and history makers | Includes index. | Audience: Grades 4-6.
Identifiers: LCCN 2020001017 (print) | LCCN 2020001018 (ebook) | ISBN
    9781496684752 (hardcover) | ISBN 9781496688170 (paperback) | ISBN
    9781496684950 (pdf)
Subjects: LCSH: Kelly, Scott, 1964—Juvenile literature. | International
    Space Station—Juvenile literature. | Astronauts—United
    States—Biography—Juvenile literature. | Space environment—Juvenile
    literature.
Classification: LCC TL789.85.K45 S29 2021 (print) | LCC TL789.85.K45
    (ebook) | DDC 629.450092 [B]—dc23
LC record available at https://lccn.loc.gov/2020001017
LC ebook record available at https://lccn.loc.gov/2020001018

Image Credits
iStockphoto: 4nadia, 7, rglinsky, 11; NASA: Ben Smegelsky/KSC, 30, Bill Ingalls/HQ, 5, 8, 39, 43, JSC, 17, 19, 20, 23, 31 (space station), 35, 37, Kim Shiflett/KSC, 40, Kjell Lindgren/JSC, 28, NASA Goddard/GSFC, 15, Robert Markowitz, cover (foreground), 25, Scott Kelly/JSC, 32, 34, Victor Zelentsov/HQ, 27; Red Line Editorial: 12, 31 (map); Shutterstock Images: muratart, cover (background), 1

Editorial Credits
Editor: Charly Haley; Designer: Colleen McLaren; Production Specialist: Ryan Gale

Printed in the United States of America.
PA117

CONTENTS

Words in **bold** are in the glossary.

CHAPTER ONE

EARLY LIFE

When Scott Kelly was a kid, he never thought about being an astronaut. But he knew that he liked taking risks. Kelly and his twin brother, Mark, got a thrill from anything scary or dangerous. They climbed to the roof of their house. They went sailing on the ocean in an unsafe boat. When their engine died and the boat began filling with water, they had to be rescued. But Kelly wasn't bothered by this. He was excited by the challenge.

Scott and Mark Kelly were born on February 21, 1964. Their parents were both police officers. The family lived in Orange, New Jersey.

When Scott Kelly was young, no one would have expected him to become a record-setting astronaut one day. He was not a great student.

Scott Kelly (left) and his twin brother, Mark Kelly, both grew up to become astronauts.

He didn't get good grades. Instead of paying attention in class, he would stare out the window.

FINDING PURPOSE

When Kelly was in high school, his grades didn't get better. But he did find a thrilling new job. After he turned 16, Kelly became an emergency medical technician (EMT). When people called 911 with an emergency, Kelly rode in an ambulance to help them. Kelly loved this job. He thrived in scary situations where he had to react quickly.

After high school, Kelly went to college. In his first year, he wasn't motivated. But then Kelly read a book called *The Right Stuff*. It changed everything for him. The book was about test pilots and astronauts. It described how pilots risked their lives as they flew planes. Kelly was very interested in this.

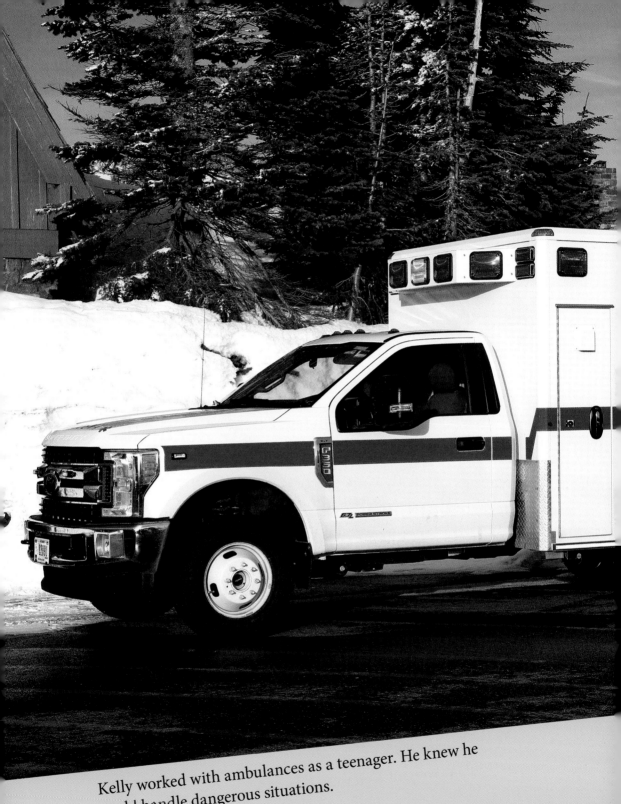

Kelly worked with ambulances as a teenager. He knew he could handle dangerous situations.

When Kelly read the book about pilots, he did not know that it would eventually lead to his becoming an astronaut.

He read about the daring things these pilots did. The pilots faced challenges that seemed impossible. Kelly wanted to be like them.

After Kelly read that book, he decided to change colleges and join the military. He was going to become a pilot. Maybe he would even become an astronaut.

CHAPTER TWO

EXPLORING THE SKIES

Kelly changed colleges so he could pursue his new dream. He went to Maritime College State University of New York. Kelly had to learn how to study. He needed to get good grades if he wanted to become a pilot. He had to work hard at math and science. Even though his classes were tough, Kelly didn't give up. He stayed focused on his dream. His work paid off. After graduating, he joined the U.S. Navy.

Kelly began training to become a navy pilot. The training was very difficult. It prepared pilots for emergencies they might face. In one part of training, Kelly had to climb into a pretend helicopter. The helicopter was dropped into a pool. It began to sink. Kelly had to find his way out. This was very stressful. But it was important if Kelly was going to be prepared for a plane crash in real life.

Kelly studied hard at his new college to become a pilot for the
U.S. Navy.

When he was in the navy, Kelly sailed all over the world. He saw the North Atlantic Ocean, the Mediterranean Sea, the Red Sea, and the Persian Gulf.

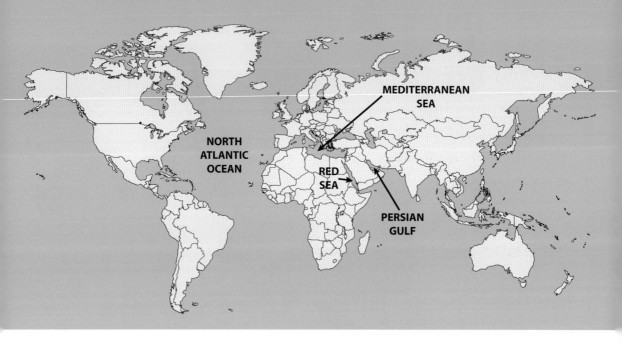

The training also taught Kelly to be an expert pilot. Flying planes in the navy is very challenging. Navy pilots don't have long runways for landings like at airports. Instead, they have to land planes on moving ships. Kelly had to practice for many hours before he mastered this skill. Kelly also got his master's degree in aviation systems. He learned about different types of planes and how they work.

Once Kelly was an expert at flying planes, he became a test pilot. He got to try out new planes and flight technology to make sure everything worked correctly. When he tested new equipment, no one could predict what might go wrong. Kelly was very excited about this job. He was doing the same work as the pilots in the book that inspired him. His risky, daring flights could save lives.

Eventually Kelly decided to try something new. A lot of his friends were applying to become astronauts. His brother, Mark, who was also a navy pilot, was applying. Kelly decided to try it too. He went through a challenging interview. The interviewers checked his eyesight. They checked how healthy his heart was. They even checked how **claustrophobic** he was! Kelly was worried he wouldn't meet the requirements. That would mean he wouldn't be able to become an astronaut.

After the interview, Kelly waited and waited. After six months, he finally got the call. He was going to be an astronaut at the National Aeronautics and Space Administration (NASA). His brother was too!

BECOMING AN ASTRONAUT

After he accepted the job offer, Kelly still had more learning to do. Astronauts have to understand how the **space shuttle** works. They have to be prepared for any emergency. They have to know how to repair equipment. Kelly spent lots of time learning and practicing. Three years after he started working with NASA, he got the opportunity to go to space. He was going to fix the Hubble **Telescope**. The Hubble Telescope **orbits** Earth. It uses powerful telescopes to help NASA see far into outer space. It takes pictures. Scientists study the pictures to learn more about space and Earth.

As Kelly got ready to go to space for the first time, bad weather and mechanical problems delayed his space shuttle's launch. Kelly didn't like waiting.

The Hubble Telescope is very powerful. NASA has used it to look very far into space.

He was too excited! Finally the weather cleared up, and the space shuttle blasted off into space. Kelly was amazed. He saw the sun rising above Earth. For eight days, Kelly lived in the tiny space shuttle. He spent Christmas looking down at Earth. Kelly couldn't believe that he was living out his dreams.

THE INTERNATIONAL SPACE STATION

After Kelly's space flight, NASA began working with other countries to build something new. It would be called the International Space Station. The space station would be an important place for astronauts. It would let astronauts be in space for much longer than they could on a space shuttle. Astronauts would be able to live on the space station. They could do science experiments. They could learn more about how to live in space.

But building the space station was going to be difficult. It was going to be as long as a football field. It was so big, it needed to be put together in space.

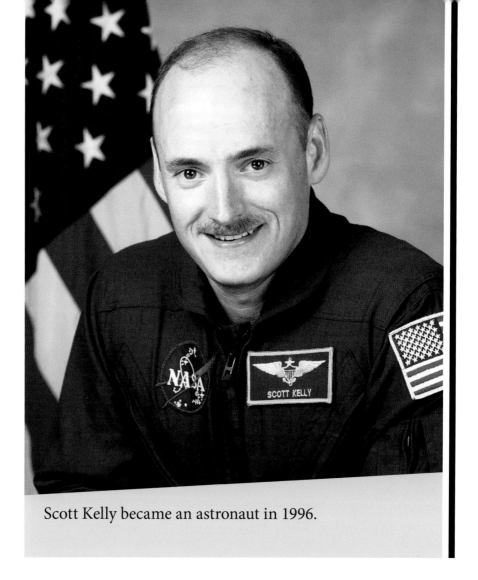

Scott Kelly became an astronaut in 1996.

The space station was too expensive and too much work for one country. American astronauts needed to work with other countries. So Kelly moved to Russia. He worked with Russian scientists to plan the space station. Kelly also led a team of astronauts that flew into space in 2007 and helped build the space station.

WHAT DOES IT TAKE TO BE AN ASTRONAUT?

It is very hard to become an astronaut like Kelly. Would you like to be an astronaut? Here are some of the things that you'll need:

- A COLLEGE DEGREE IN ENGINEERING, SCIENCE, OR MATH

- THREE YEARS OF RELATED WORK EXPERIENCE OR 1,000 HOURS FLYING AN AIRPLANE

- STRONG HEALTH, INCLUDING EXCELLENT VISION

- ASTRONAUT CANDIDATES MUST ALSO HAVE SKILLS IN LEADERSHIP, TEAMWORK, AND COMMUNICATION. HAVING EXPERIENCE WITH SCUBA DIVING, WILDERNESS SURVIVAL, AND LANGUAGES HELPS ASTRONAUTS TOO!

As the leader, Kelly had to make important decisions. When the space shuttle launched, part of its outer covering fell off. Returning to Earth would be dangerous without it. Kelly had to work with others to decide what to do. He could try to land the shuttle, even with the damage. Or he could try to fix the shuttle in space.

But the repairs would be challenging. They might not work. If they went wrong, it could put the crew in more danger! But Kelly stayed calm. He read research from teams at NASA. He decided not to fix the shuttle. During the landing, the team was nervous.

The International Space Station allows astronauts to conduct research in space.

Kelly had fun with other crew members on the International Space Station.

But Kelly landed the space shuttle safely. Everyone was relieved. Kelly had made the right decision.

Then Kelly got another opportunity. NASA asked him to live on the International Space Station for six months with astronauts from around the world.

At first, Kelly wasn't sure if he wanted to do it. He liked flying into space. But he had never planned on living there. He decided to accept the mission anyway. He started training to live in space. He traveled all over the world for training. He worked with astronauts from Russia, Germany, and Japan.

Kelly had fun living on the space station in 2010. But he also faced challenges. It was hard for him to be away from his family. Kelly didn't know it yet, but his experience in space would bring a bigger opportunity.

ASTRONAUTS IN THE OCEAN

Space isn't the only interesting place that Kelly has lived. He also lived in the ocean! In 2002, Kelly led Operation NEEMO 4. For five days, a crew of astronauts lived 62 feet (19 meters) under the ocean's surface. They did experiments, practiced skills they would need for space missions, and learned how to live in a small place. This helped them prepare for life on the International Space Station.

CHAPTER THREE

A YEAR IN SPACE

After 19 years as an astronaut, Kelly got the chance of a lifetime. NASA asked him to spend a year on the International Space Station. Astronauts had only ever lived on the space station for six months at a time. No one had ever lived there for nearly a year.

This mission had a special purpose. NASA hopes to send people to Mars one day. But the journey to Mars would probably take many months. Scientists wanted to learn what might happen to humans if they spent that much time in space. Kelly's mission was going to help answer that question.

Kelly was nervous about being away from his family for so long. But he decided to accept the mission. Kelly and his Russian teammate would spend 340 days on the space station.

Kelly took many photos, such as this selfie, to document his time in space.

Kelly would see what happens to a person's body after all that time in space. His findings would help astronauts prepare for a trip to Mars.

THE TWIN STUDY

Researchers planned to study Kelly's whole body while he was in space. They would measure how his brain, bones, muscles, and **cells** changed. Cells are the tiny building blocks that make up all living things, including human bodies. Researchers really wanted to study Kelly's **genes**. Genes carry very important information in cells. They tell cells how a person's body should grow.

Kelly was perfect for this mission because he has an identical twin brother, Mark Kelly. Identical twins have identical genes. Scientists would study Kelly's and his brother's genes.

Researchers compared differences between Scott Kelly (right) and Mark Kelly to understand the effects of living in space for a long time.

While Kelly lived in space, his brother would stay on Earth. They would both do the same tests. If both of their bodies changed in the same ways, the scientists would know that the changes were normal. If only Kelly's body changed, scientists could guess that it was because he was in space.

Kelly and two Russian teammates blasted off on March 27, 2015. His teammate Mikhail Kornienko would stay with him in space for the whole year, while the other Russian teammate would leave after six months. Kelly knew he was setting off on a very important mission. But it was also dangerous.

LIFE ON THE SPACE STATION

Life on the International Space Station is very different from life on Earth! Did you know...

- ASTRONAUTS DON'T SLEEP IN BEDS. THEY STRAP THEMSELVES INTO SLEEPING BAGS ATTACHED TO THE WALL!

- WHEN ASTRONAUTS GO TO THE BATHROOM, THEIR URINE GETS FILTERED AND RECYCLED INTO DRINKING WATER.

- ASTRONAUTS CAN'T USE REGULAR SALT AND PEPPER. WITHOUT GRAVITY, THE FLAKES WOULD JUST FLOAT AWAY! THEY HAVE TO SPREAD LIQUID SALT AND PEPPER ON THEIR FOOD.

- ASTRONAUTS CAN'T EAT ANY FOOD THAT MAKES CRUMBS. MOST OF THEIR FOOD COMES SEALED IN A POUCH.

No one knew what might happen to him. Would he get sick? Could his body stay healthy in space?

WORKING ON THE INTERNATIONAL SPACE STATION

After six hours in the **spacecraft**, Kelly and his teammates arrived at the International Space Station. They had a lot of work to do.

The Soyuz TMA-16M spacecraft brought Kelly and his teammates to the International Space Station.

One of Kelly's jobs was to help keep the space station running. It is always orbiting Earth 250 miles (400 km) above the planet's surface. It travels at 17,500 mph (28,100 kmh). That means it goes around Earth once in just 90 minutes! It never comes down to the ground for repairs. The astronauts on board need to make sure the station runs smoothly at all times.

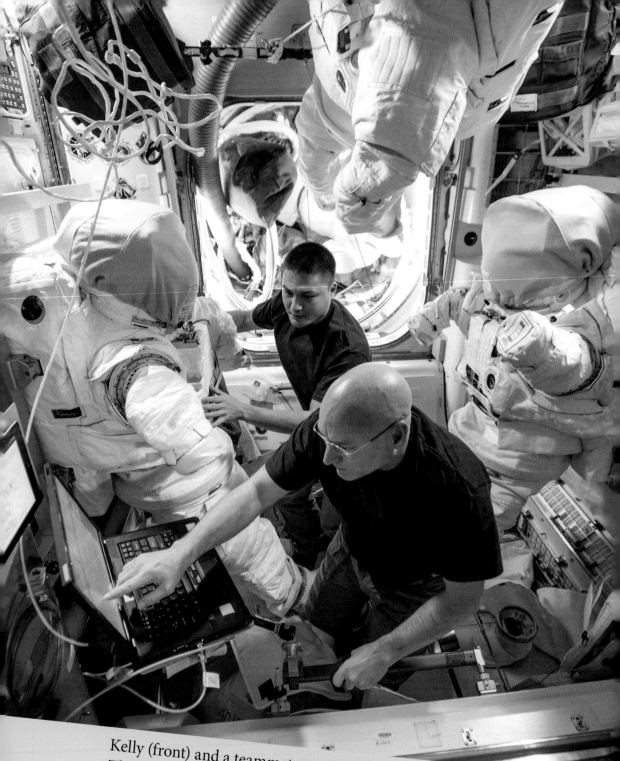

Kelly (front) and a teammate prepared for a spacewalk. They made sure their spacesuits and other equipment were working correctly.

Sometimes Kelly or his teammates had to go outside the space station to make repairs. This is called a spacewalk. During a spacewalk, astronauts put on a high-tech space suit. The space suit helps protect them from the dangerously hot and cold temperatures of space. It also gives them oxygen to breathe and water to drink. Astronauts put on the suit long before they go outside. This way their bodies can adjust to the suit. Then they go through a special door to leave the safety of the space station. Kelly did three spacewalks to make repairs during his year in space.

Kelly also helped with science experiments in space. When Kelly landed on the space station, the crew was already trying to grow plants. Their goal was to grow food that could be eaten on a long flight. Before Kelly arrived, astronauts had already learned to grow lettuce there. Kelly's crew got a new challenge. They started growing flowers called zinnias. When the flowers began to get moldy and die, Kelly took charge of the space garden. He helped astronauts learn about how to make sure plants get enough water and light in space.

Zinnias growing in the International Space Station

Kelly helped with the science experiments on himself too. These were the experiments that involved studying his body and comparing it with his brother on Earth. Kelly did all kinds of tests on himself to see how his body changed in space. He drew his own blood. He gave himself shots. He took samples of his urine and poop.

Being in space made these tests tricky. If Kelly took a blood sample, he didn't have much time before the sample went bad. He had to give it to a crew just before they left the space station to go back to Earth.

DELIVERING KELLY'S BLOOD SAMPLES

Kelly's blood had to travel a long way for scientists to study it. The blood was delivered from outer space and across the world!

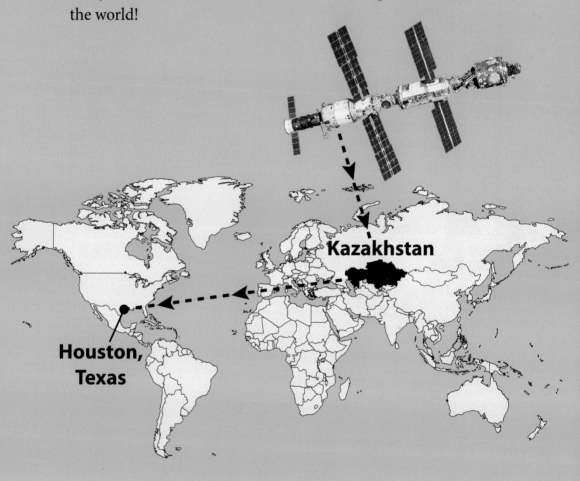

Kazakhstan

Houston,
Texas

The crew landed in Kazakhstan, where scientists collected the samples. They immediately shipped the samples to a lab across the world in Houston, Texas.

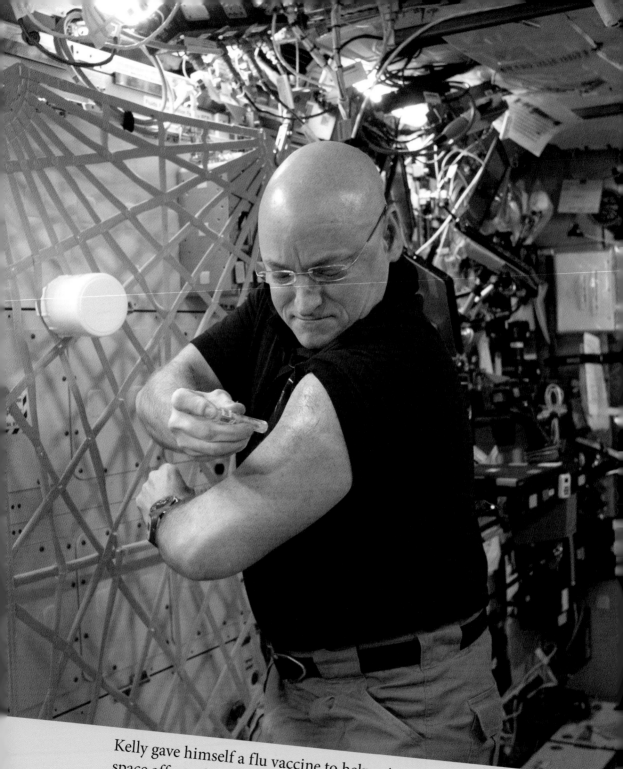

Kelly gave himself a flu vaccine to help scientists study how space affects the immune system.

Within 48 hours after Kelly drew his blood, it would be studied by scientists back on Earth.

LIFE IN SPACE

During his year in space, Kelly experienced some amazing things. He saw incredible views of Earth. He took beautiful pictures of the oceans, the Northern Lights, and New York City at night. He got to see a sunset and sunrise every 45 minutes. He also got to have some fun. His brother sent him a gorilla suit. Kelly put on the suit and made a funny video chasing his teammate around the space station.

But living in space was also difficult. Kelly and his teammate relied on supply spacecraft to bring them food and equipment for experiments. Sometimes these spacecraft had problems. One of them exploded when it took off.

Another one couldn't make it to the space station. All the supplies on both spacecraft were destroyed. Kelly and his teammate started to worry. They might not have the right supplies for experiments.

Kelly photographed the Northern Lights during his year in space.

Kelly worked a lot while living and traveling in space.

They were also counting on the spacecraft to bring them more food. Thankfully, they didn't run out of food before the next supply spacecraft made it to the space station.

While he was in space, Kelly sometimes wished he could have a normal day. In space, he couldn't start his morning with a warm shower. Instead, he used special soap that didn't need much water. He didn't get to set his own schedule. This is because NASA needs astronauts to do certain jobs at certain times.

Kelly also had to fit in more than two hours of exercise every day. He ran and lifted weights so his muscles wouldn't weaken. Kelly also missed his family. He could email his girlfriend and daughters. He talked to them on the phone sometimes too. But he couldn't hug them or chat with them every night.

Kelly was grateful to spend most of a year in space. But when his 340 days on the International Space Station ended, he was ready to head home.

KELLY'S SOCIAL MEDIA

While he was in space, Kelly shared his life through social media. For National Burger Day, he posted pictures of a "space burger." It was a burger heated in hot water, wrapped in a tortilla, and topped with cheese spread, ketchup, and mustard. He shared an image of the crew watching the movie *The Martian*. On Valentine's Day, he snapped images of the flowers he grew in space. Lots of people enjoyed following his posts. Even U.S. President Barack Obama commented on some of Kelly's posts!

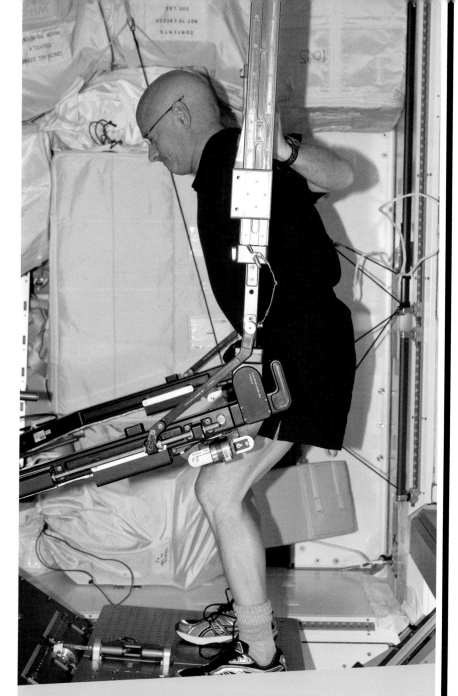

Kelly exercised on the International Space Station. It is important for astronauts to exercise while they are in space to keep their bones and muscles healthy.

CHAPTER FOUR

BACK ON EARTH

When Kelly finally returned to Earth at the end of the year, his important job wasn't over. He continued to do medical tests. Those medical tests revealed some interesting information.

One change doctors noticed was that Kelly grew 2 inches (5 centimeters) while he was in space. His body had stretched out because **gravity** was not pulling it downward. However, those changes didn't last. He soon returned to his normal height back on Earth.

Kelly's eyes were also affected by space. His vision became worse. Living in space makes it harder for some astronauts to see things clearly and can cause headaches. Scientists are working on ways to prevent it.

After Kelly's year in space, he continued working on the project by going through medical tests and helping researchers.

HOW DID A YEAR IN SPACE AFFECT KELLY'S BODY?

KELLY GREW 2 INCHES (5 CM) IN SPACE.

KELLY'S GENES CHANGED IN SPACE.

LIVING IN SPACE MADE KELLY'S VISION BLURRIER.

Kelly's genes also changed. Scientists still don't know why this happened. They're still paying attention to how these changes affect Kelly.

Kelly and his brother will continue to be studied for the rest of their lives. But Kelly says it's worth it. He gets to help astronauts keep learning. He believes he can help make a trip to Mars possible someday.

RETIREMENT FROM NASA

Shortly after Kelly returned to Earth, he retired from NASA. He said it was time to give other astronauts a turn.

But he has continued sharing information about his incredible year in space. He wrote a book about his life. He made a picture book about being an astronaut too.

He published a collection of the photographs he took from space. He was also featured in a documentary.

Kelly wants to help other people become astronauts. He likes talking about his experiences. He wants all kids to know that they can learn math, science, and engineering. Maybe they could even be part of an astronaut team that goes to Mars. Thanks to Kelly's work, that trip might really happen someday!

RECORD TIME IN SPACE

During his year in space, Kelly set a record for the most days spent in space in a row by an American astronaut. But Kelly doesn't want to keep his records. He hopes that someone else will break them. He wants other astronauts to continue working and trying new things!

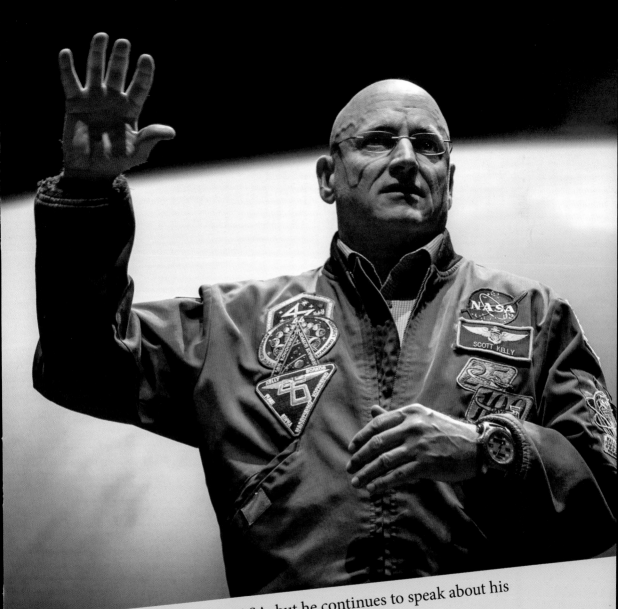

Kelly retired from NASA, but he continues to speak about his experiences in space to help people learn.

TIMELINE

1964: Scott Kelly is born.

1982: Kelly graduates from high school.

1987: Kelly graduates from college with a bachelor's degree in electrical engineering.

1989: Kelly becomes a pilot with the U.S. Navy.

1993: Kelly becomes a test pilot and tests new planes and software.

1996: Kelly graduates with a master's degree in aviation systems.

1996: Kelly becomes an astronaut.

1999: Kelly goes to space for the first time to repair the Hubble Telescope.

2007: Kelly goes to space to help build the International Space Station.

2010: Kelly spends 6 months living in space on board the International Space Station.

2015: Kelly sets a record by living for nearly a year on the International Space Station.

2016: Kelly retires from NASA.

2017: Kelly publishes a book about his life and his year in space.

GLOSSARY

cells (SELS)
the smallest units of a
living thing

**claustrophobic
(klawss-truh-FOH-bic)**
having a fear of small,
cramped spaces

genes (JEENS)
tiny parts of a cell that
can act like instructions
for how cells should
grow; genes are passed
down from parents
to children

gravity (GRAV-uh-tee)
a force that pulls objects
with mass together;
gravity pulls objects
down toward the center
of Earth

orbit (OR-bit)
to travel around an object
in space

**spacecraft
(SPAYSS-kraft)**
a vehicle that travels
in space

**space shuttle
(SPAYSS SHUHT-uhl)**
a spacecraft that carried
astronauts and cargo to
outer space and returned
to Earth when its mission
was complete; space
shuttles were used from
1981–2011

**telescope
(TEL-uh-skohp)**
a tool that makes faraway
objects seem larger
and closer

READ MORE

Jenkins, Martin. *Exploring Space: From Galileo to the Mars Rover and Beyond*. Somerville, MA: Candlewick Press, 2017.

Kelly, Scott, and Margaret Lazarus Dean. *Endurance: My Year in Space and How I Got There*. Young Readers Edition. New York: Crown Books, 2018.

Spilsbury, Richard. *Space*. North Mankato, MN: Capstone Press, 2019.

INTERNET SITES

NASA Kids Club
https://www.nasa.gov/kidsclub/index.html

NASA Space Place
https://spaceplace.nasa.gov/

National Geographic Kids: Passport to Space
https://kids.nationalgeographic.com/explore/space/passport-to-space/

INDEX